Stock Market Lingo

A Companion to

Confessions of a Day Trader: A Fact as Fiction Financial Thriller; Madness and Mayhem 1999-2008

By

Lloyd R. Free

SUGARHILL PRESS
Reno, NV

ISBN-13: 978-1-948664-01-1

INTRODUCTION

"One of the funny things about the stock market is that every time one person buys, another sells, and both think they are astute." - William Feather

"Lesson number one. Don't underestimate the other guy's greed."— "Scarface" (1983)

After 10 years of actively trading the stock market (24/7)—live trades haunt weekends—I was exhausted and needed a break. I had learned a great deal about human nature and about myself. It had been a thrilling ride. In fact, I felt like a Marine returning from battling jihadists in Iraq: the first decade of the 21st century featured the financially bloody Dot Com bubble burst, the 9/11 disaster, the 2008 world financial crisis; daily bursts of deadly gunfire from the Market Makers; and insiders, the smart money, manipulating the market to fleece the outsiders, the retail investor. After the dust had settled and my PTSD had faded, I felt my adventures deserved to be put to paper for the benefit of

1

other would-be day traders and anyone interested in experiencing what it would be like to trade the markets.

When I first conceived the *fact as fiction novel,* **Confessions of a Day Trader,** I believed my audience would be primarily day traders, financial gurus and wealthy investors. I believed most readers would be familiar with stock market terms the use of which was required to realistically describe the events being portrayed. This was certainly the case with most of my fans:

"Based on a true story this is a fantastic book about what it's really like in the investment arena. A behind the scenes look at what life is like and the crazy ups and downs. If you are a fan of movies about the stock market this is a sure bet." by Buzz (Amazon Review).

And:

"I was about to turn this book away thinking it was a guide but this is a story and an interesting one at that. Great look at the ups and downs of a real day trader. Lessons learned and a lot of money thrown away!" by Natalla Escobar (Amazon Review).

But then there were others only marginally familiar with the stock market who protested the use of stock market jargon:

"A lot of technical jargon made this book not as fun to read as I thought that it would." by Logan (Goodreads Review)

I took to heart Logan's complaint but knew I could not write about the stock market, at least realistically, without exposing jargon and strategies used by Wall Street and retail investors. Hence my dilemma. What could I do to give the novice a few tools that might help him more easily experience the daily wild ride of the day trader the better to enjoy Jay and Stevy's plight. After some thought, I came to the conclusion that a short introduction to trader jargon and trading strategies including definitions and examples might help.

This primer is not meant for the experienced trader. It is not intended to be a manual on day trading since it only touches the terms used in the novel and excludes all other relevant material relating to stock market activity. It is meant to be a very quick read for my fans to facilitate their reading experience.

Lexicon

The stock market

I am sure that almost everyone has heard the word stock market. The term is bandied about but what is it really? In essence, it is nothing more than a bazaar where things are bought and sold. A place where a seller asks a price and a buyer bids a price. It could be an open-air or an indoor auction hall. It is a place where debt is bought and sold. The basic product of this market place is a stock or equity, an ownership position in some sort of business enterprise. Why did the stock market come about? Let's say a person starts a business. He will need capital.

He could go to a bank to borrow money, but most banks are conservative and will not risk capital on a new venture.

He could go to a private lender or a loan shark, but interest rates would probably be astronomical and broken kneecaps common.

A third alternative is to offer a stake in the enterprise in exchange for money—a sort of loan collateralized by a piece of the action. The lender (otherwise known as investor) risks his money betting that the new enterprise will thrive. At this point in the game, the stock or share in the company is privately held. The holder can sell his stock if he chooses and if he can find a private buyer. What would make that task easier? Why a club where buyers and sellers meet.

The Belgians created the first "exchange" in the 16th century where they "made a market" in promissory notes. From this humble beginning evolved today's complex stock market; however, the basic idea of trading in debt (a stock is a loan backed by the collateral of the value of the entity) continues. If the business succeeds the lender (stockholder) makes money as the value of his share in the company rises; if the business fails, the lender (stockholder) can lose his entire investment as the stock price falls. Over the decades these private security exchanges evolved into public trading houses called **exchanges**. If the stockholders possessing private shares in a private company needed more capital, they could create new shares out of thin air and offer them to the public through stock exchanges. The major public stock exchanges in the United States are the NYSE (New York Stock Exchange), the NASDAQ (First fully computerized trading exchange designed to replace the "specialists" at the NYSE and AMEX), AMEX (mainly ETFs or Exchange Traded Funds); the OTC (Over the Counter) and Pink Sheet stocks, the CBOE (Chicago Board of Options Exchange). Each of these exchanges specializes in certain stocks (the stocks listed on the exchange). Today most stock transactions are computerized—trading is done over digital platforms.

The Players

- **Big Money or Smart Money**: institutional investors such as mutual funds, market mavens, hedge fund managers and financial experts. The smart money represents the well-informed—insiders, people well connected and "in the know." Warren Buffett is an example of the smart money and his Berkshire Hathaway can easily move the price of a stock just by taking a position in a company.

- **Dumb money**: retail investors who are not in the know and have no insider information about which stocks will rise and which stocks will fall. In the ebb and the flow of the markets, the smart money usually sells its equities to the dumb money when the market reaches its peak and then buys those shares back after a market correction.

- **Market Makers**: these cute little creatures are the bane of the retail investor. A Market Maker is a company such as a brokerage house which acts as a sort of wholesaler of equities buying and selling them in order to provide liquidity in the markets. The justification for Market Makers is that they are entrusted with promoting market efficiency by keeping markets liquid. Market Makers make money from the spread between the bid and the ask. In addition, if they are a brokerage house, they will charge a fee for a trade. While it is true that Market Makers create liquidity, they are also in the business of making money for themselves—often employing a bevy of questionable techniques. Since they control to a large extent the bid and the ask especially at the open (see the definition of gap up and gap down) and the price of options (see the discussion of options) the Market Makers can manipulate the price of stocks working the markets to their advantage at the expense of their clients. For example, if a Market Maker is a brokerage house, it can front run trades which simply means that they place orders for their own account ahead of the orders for their clients. This is particularly true in volatile markets when stocks are rising or falling at unusual speed. _Confessions_ *Pg. 142-144, 167-168, 170, 200, 223.*

- **Brokerage houses:** a brokerage firm acts as an agent in purchases or sales in return for a fee or commission. A brokerage house may offer financial advice to its clients as well as being the intermediary in the trading of stocks. It may also act as a lending institution in so far as it can set up a margin account which allows a customer to borrow money to buy stock. A margin account is somewhat like a commercial bank line of credit collateralized by receivables. In this case, the collateral is the value of a customer's stock portfolio. Depending on the customer's net worth and portfolio, the trading department of the brokerage house will determine the ratio of collateral required to borrow money. A common ratio might be 45% collateral (the current dollar value of the stocks held in the customer's account) and 55% margin (margin stands for the amount of available credit). This line of credit is a positive in so far as it allows a trader to purchase stocks well beyond his available capital. However, buying on margin can be very dangerous for two reasons. Number one, the value of the stocks in the trader's portfolio may decline to a point where the collateral is worth less than the margin money lent by the brokerage house. Number two, the brokerage house can change the margin ratios at any time. This means that if a stock or stocks are falling in value, the brokerage house can arbitrarily change the ratio and issue a margin call. The trader has three days to come up with the money demanded by the brokerage house. If the trader does not have the capital, then the brokerage house has the legal right to sell off enough shares to cover the unpaid margin debt. A trader is margined out when he has borrowed up to his limit. *Confessions pg.142*

- **Discount brokerage houses**: in general, a brokerage firm that does not offer financial advice or financial products. Its sole function is to act as an agent for buying and selling stocks for which they charge a commission. With the advent of computerized stock trading platforms, discount brokerage houses were born such as Scottrade, Trade Station, Interactive Brokers, and E*TRADE. These brokerage houses charge as little as five dollars a trade making it possible for the retail investor, the average person, to trade without the high commissions that were common in the 1960s and 70s. Before their creation, only the wealthy could afford to play the stock markets. These new computerized brokerage platforms democratized the markets. _Confessions_ **Pg. 132**

- **Mutual fund**: An investment vehicle made up of a pool of monies collected from many investors for the purpose of investing in stocks, bonds, and money markets. Mutual funds are registered and operated by professional money managers, who allocate the fund's investments and attempt to produce capital gains for investors. Mutual Funds cannot take short positions.

- **Hedge Funds:** An investment vehicle made up of a pool of monies collected from many investors for the purpose of investing in stocks, bonds, and other financial instruments. It began as a type of private and unregistered investment pool that employed sophisticated hedging and arbitrage techniques to trade in the corporate equity markets. Hedge funds have traditionally been limited to sophisticated, wealthy investors. In earlier markets, the term "hedge fund" referred to an asset class employing a strategy to offset its market risk exposure by taking an opposing position – for example, selling short or holding futures. Today, a hedge fund can be just about anything because, over time, the activities of hedge funds broadened into other financial instruments and activities. Today, the term "hedge fund" refers not so much to hedging techniques, which hedge funds may or may not employ, as it does to their status as private and unregistered investment pools. They generally only accept financially sophisticated, high-net-worth investors. Some funds are limited to no more than 100 investors. *Confessions pg.49, 81, 129, 177, 185*

Investment vehicles

- **Common stock**: a claim on profits in the form of dividends and confers voting rights. Stockholders usually get one vote per share owned to elect board members who oversee the major decisions made by the management of a company. The investor makes money by means of capital growth—the company grows in value and the price of the stock rises. If a company goes bankrupt and liquidates, the common shareholders will not receive money until the creditors, bondholders and preferred stockholders are paid. Usually, a company bankruptcy wipes out the value of common stock. *Confessions pg. 147-151.*

- **Preferred Stock**: this financial instrument is similar to a bond in that investors are guaranteed a fixed dividend. In the event of a bankruptcy, the preferred shareholders are paid off before the common shareholders after the other debtholders and creditors have been paid.

- **Options:** a stock option is a contract between two parties giving one party the right to buy or sell a stock at an agreed-upon price within a certain period of time. The purchaser of the option is not obligated to exercise the option before the expiration date. Stock options are liquid and trade like stocks. An options contract normally represents 100 shares of an underlying stock. The investor in the option must take into account the option price, the strike price and the expiration date. Stock options have been called a poor man's stock since the price of an option can be very low relative to the price of the underlying stock. Two basic stock options are available: a **call option**—when a trader enters into a contract to purchase a stock at a specific price at a specific date; a **put option**—when a trader enters into a contract to sell a stock at an agreed price on or before a specific date. A call option is a bet that the stock price will rise. As it does, the price of the option increases. A put option is a bet that the price of the underlying equity will decline. In both cases timeframe is critical—as the expiration date approaches the value of the option decreases due to **time decay**. The strike price is the predetermined price that the underlying stock can be bought or sold. Call option traders profit when the strike price is lower than the market value of the underlying equity and put option traders profit when the strike price is higher than the current market value of the underlying equity. _Confessions_ *pg.141,148,158,198,200-212,250*

- **Blue Chip Stocks**: well-established and financially sound nationally recognized companies. They are large companies whose products are widely used. They have stable growth and usually pay regular dividends. Examples would be IBM, General Electric, Coca-Cola, and DuPont.

- **Pink Sheet Stocks**: small-company stocks traded over-the-counter. They are also known as penny stocks since many if not most trade for under a dollar. These stocks are extremely volatile and can be affected by news or rumor such as a fake press release. *Confessions* **pg. 150, 166, 170**

Buy/Sell Order Types

- **market order:**. It is the most basic type of buy or sell order and it simply requests that the brokerage house execute an entire trade at the prevailing market prices. If the trader is wishing to buy an equity, the trade will generally go through at the ask price and if he wishes to sell, the order will go through at the bid price. The problem with a market order is that quotes are based on the last successful trade and, due to what is called **slippage,** the trader may receive a price much less than the bid or the ask price. This is particularly the case if an equity's price is volatile or if the trader is dealing in an illiquid stock, that is to say, a stock with a very small **float** (the float is the number of shares actually available for trade). Oftentimes, small companies with let's say 20 million shares outstanding may have only 1 million or less that are available for trading.

- **limit order**: it is a type of order to simply execute a trade at a certain price. This sounds simple enough but the trader's order may never go through if there are no shares available at the specified price or the order may only be partially filled. In fact, limit orders may give the Market Makers the opportunity, when it is to their advantage, to play with the price action so that the limit order never gets filled.

- **stop order**: it sets a price floor for an equity. The trader is ordering a market sell order if the stock reaches a certain price either above or below its current price. It is intended to lock in a profit if the price rises or to limit losses if a stock price drops.

There are other types of orders which we will not discuss: a trailing stop, conditional orders, GTC orders, AON orders.

- **Short Selling** or Shorting a Stock: when a trader believes that a stock price will decline, he can short the stock. The idea of shorting is a little complicated but it boils down to the following: the short seller "borrows" the stock from a broker, and immediately sells the stock at its current market price, with the sale proceeds credited to the short seller's margin account. At a future point in time, the short seller will buy back the stock, return the "borrowed" stock to the broker and pay back the amount borrowed to purchase the short position. Convoluted, yes. Most financial experts consider shorting a dangerous practice since a short position has, theoretically, unlimited risk.
Confessions **Pg. 70, 194, 198, 204, 207, 211, 221-222, 228.**

Types of Trading

- **Day trading**: very short-term trades based on tight time frames. A few days at the most.

- **Swing trading**: trades lasting over a few weeks.

- **Long-term investing**: buying stocks to hold for a year or more. In particular, dividend stocks, blue-chip stocks with very low volatility.

Fundamental Analysis versus Technical Analysis

- **Fundamental Analysis** evaluates businesses to determine their suitability for investment. Fundamental Analysis is used to analyze whether an entity is stable, solvent, liquid, and profitable; it looks at the quarterly and year-end financial reports as well as the financial projections issued by management. If a business is not doing well, management may try to fudge the numbers. One way is to show profit as EBITA (earnings before interest, taxes, depreciation and amortization). The eliminated items can be factors that distort earnings and make the company's earnings appear greater. Warren Buffett uses Fundamental Analysis for long term bets.

- **Technical Analysis**: technical analysis only looks at the price movement of a security and uses this data to predict future price movements. Most day traders and swing traders rely on technical analysis. It consists of charts and indicators derived from price movements and mathematical ratios. What follows is an abbreviated list of the tools of Technical Analysis.

- **Charts**: A graphic display of stock price movements. By graphing price action the trader can look for price patterns which may repeat predicting future price action. Chart time frames can be changed the better to zoom in or zoom out on a stock's performance— one minute, five minute, one hour, one day, one week, one month, one year or a hundred years.

- **Bar Chart:** composed of vertical lines—each representing the highest and the lowest price for the time frame charted.

- **Candlestick Chart:** each data point or candle is composed of a wide line and two short lines, the former is called the body and the latter the wicks. Each candle formation shows four principal data points—the opening price, the closing price, the high of the day and the low of the day. Certain formations have Japanese names such as dogi, harami; some names have been translated into English—hammers, gravestones, shooting stars. Each formation is supposed to predict a future price move. A bar chart works best for longer periods and candlesticks work very well for shorter time frames.

The illustration that follows shows the very graphic nature of the Japanese Candlestick Chart.

NIAL FULLER *Professional Trader, Author & Trading Coach*

Confessions Pg. 142,145, 175-176, 207-208.

- **Technical Indicators** Technical indicators are mathematical calculations based on a stock's past and present price or volume activity. Technical analysts use historical performance to predict future prices. A trader must interpret the signals to determine when to buy and when to sell. (See "Introduction to Stock Trading Indicators". The link is listed below). http://stockcharts.com/school/doku.php?id=chart_scho ol:technical_indicators:introduction_to_technical_indic ators_and_oscillators

The most commonly used indicators are:

- **Stochastics**: an oscillator based on ratios that show overbought and oversold market conditions. *Confessions Pg. 102, 126, 176, 224.*

- **Relative strength indicator**: A momentum investing calculation that compares the performance of a stock to that of the overall market. Relative strength calculates which equities are the strongest performers. *Confessions Pg. 102, 1766, 221-224.*

- **Advance/decline line**: Compares the amount of securities that trade higher for the day in the market compared to the amount of securities down for the day. This indicator suggests the "health" of the stock market.

- **Channels**: When charting the price of a stock, this is the area between a stocks high and low prices. The lines drawn from high to high and from low to low on the chart may form a channel. These two lines can become a stock's support and resistance levels. The price of the asset will stay within the support and resistance levels until a breakout or breakdown occurs. *Confessions pg.176*

- **Additional Trading Tools**: trends lines, moving averages, MACD, Fibonacci formulas, Bollinger Bands, to mention only a few. The mathematics creating these indicators is a science; applying indicators is an art. *Confessions pg.176*

Cycles

Analysts and historians have discovered many sorts of cycles applying to financial markets dating back to ancient times. The following list is just a sampling.

- **The business cycle** can be divided into four phases: expansion, peak, contraction, recovery. The stock market is a leading indicator of the business cycle.

- **Stock market cycle**: the stock market cycles between bull and bear markets. Harry Dent, Peter Eliades and Garrett Jones have done extensive studies of different cycles that affect the stock market: demographic patterns, spending patterns, seasonal patterns, longwave patterns.

- **The presidential cycle** relates to the American presidential cycle of four years. In an article written by Marshall Nickles ("Presidential Elections and Stock Market Cycles") the author found that all of the major stock market declines occurred during the first or second years of the four-year U.S. presidential cycle. No major declines occurred during the third or fourth years.

- **Lunar**: the eight phases of the moon are included here because some traders use astrology as an indicator for buying and selling stocks. Aside from the scientific explanation, the term "moon cycle" is often heard in astrological circles. According to astrology, the moon's cycle can affect the way we feel about things: when the moon is full or new, both males and females can experience dramatic changes in their mood and behavior. When the moon is full, stress becomes a major factor. A new moon brings with it the sense of calmness.
  Blood Red Moon: may signal a market drop of significance.
  http://www.theidiotandthemoon.com/moontrading.htmlhttp://www.theidiotandthemoon.com/moontrading.html

  Confessions Pg.251

Miscellaneous Jargon

- *Black swan:* a term coined by Nicholas Taleb. A black swan event is impossible to predict and has catastrophic effect on the stock market. *Confessions Pg. 207, 220, 221, 228.*
- *Death cross:* a death cross occurs when the short-term moving average of a security or index falls below its long-term moving average. Usually, the term refers to the 50 day moving average falling below the 200 day moving average. This signals that a stock is in a bear market. The **trend** is down and the price of the stock should continue to fall.
- **Short squeeze:** a sudden buying spree which raises the price of the stock forcing the holders of shorts to buy back stock at a price higher than what they paid for initially.

- ***Bull trap:*** A bull trap is a signal indicating that a declining trend in a stock or index has changed direction and is going up when, in fact, the stock will continue to decline.
- ***Bear trap:*** A signal that the rising trend of a stock or index has reversed when it has not. A bear trap entices traders to place shorts on the stock or index, since they expect the underlying equity to decline in value. Instead of declining, the stock price stays flat, or goes higher. <u>***Confessions***</u> ***Pg.228***
- ***Bear raid:*** The illegal practice of colluding to push a stock's price lower through concerted short selling and spreading adverse rumors about the targeted company. In a podcast which remained alive only for a day or two, Jim Cramer admitted to using this tactic when he ran his hedge fund.
- ***Gap up or gap down:*** *a change in the price of a stock from the previous day at the opening of the next trading day.* <u>***Confessions***</u> ***pg.172, 190, 199, 200, 201, 211, 212, 221-223.***
- ***IPO:*** The first sale of a stock by a private company to the public. <u>***Confessions***</u> ***Pg. 11, 16, 22, 28, 36, 42 and throughout the novel.***
- ***Moving Average:*** A stock's average price-per-share during a specific period of time. Some common time frames are 50 and 200 day moving averages.
- ***Insider trading:*** Insider trading is the buying or selling of a stock by a person who has access to material nonpublic information. Insider trading can be illegal or legal.
- **A kill order:** an order sent to a broker to cancel an order that has already been placed but has not been filled. If the trade has gone against the trader, he must place the kill order very quickly. The market maker may not honor the order until quite a bit of slippage has occurred.

- **Time decay:** this refers to trading options. The value of a call or a put option decreases due to time decay, because the probability of the stock reaching the specified strike price diminishes as the expiration date approaches.
- **A bounce:** after a rapid decline a stock may hit a temporary support level and bounce or recover. *Confessions* **pg.112,128,140,150,173,,200,213,221-229**
- **Dollar averaging:** the technique of buying more shares as the stock price rises or falls going against the trader's target. If the trend reverses then the value of the stocks purchased increases and diminishes his loss. If the trend does not reverse then the trader's loss will increase substantially. *Confessions* **pg.209**
- **Margin call:** A broker's demand on an investor using margin to deposit additional money or securities so that the margin account is brought up to the minimum maintenance margin. Margin calls occur when an account value drops below a value calculated by the broker's particular formula. The formula can change at any time based on the brokerage's trading department. *Confessions* **Pg.5, 138, 172-177, 191, 241**
- **Fibonacci Ratios:** Leonardo Fibonacci was an Italian mathematician born in 1100s. He is known to have discovered the "Fibonacci numbers,"; they are a series of numbers where each successive number is the sum of the two previous numbers. In trading, the numbers approximating 33%, 50% and 66% often become support and resistance. *Confessions* **pg. 175.**
- **DIA, SPY, QQQ:** Index Funds (An index fund is a group of securities that represents a particular segment of the market)—in this case the Dow Jones (composed of 30 equities), the S&P 500, The Nasdaq 100.

Other Sources

- ***Investopedia***
  https://www.investopedia.com/categories/tradingterms.asp
- ***Garrett Jones***
  http://www.trade2win.com/authors/546-garrett-jones
- ***Peter Eliades*** http://www.stockmarketcycles.com/
- ***Robert Prechter***
  http://stockcharts.com/school/doku.php?id=chart_school:market_analysis:elliott_wave_theory
- ***Martin Pring Japanese Candlesticks***
  https://www.amazon.com/Candlesticks-Explained-Martin-Pring-2002-06-02/dp/B01FKUD9MK/ref=sr_1_cc_4?s=aps&ie=UTF8&qid=1520108517&sr=1-4-catcorr&keywords=martin+pring+candlesticks
- ***Alexander Elder*** https://www.amazon.com/Study-Guide-_Trading-Living-Wiley-ebook/dp/B00O4Z53JU/ref=sr_1_2?s=books&ie=UTF8&qid=1520108708&sr=1-2&keywords=alexander+elder+the+new+trading+for+a+living
- ***Jerry Williams***
  https://www.amazon.com/Understanding-Minis-Trading-Jerry-Williams/dp/0934380902/ref=sr_1_1?s=books&ie=UTF8&qid=1520109173&sr=1-1&keywords=jerry+williams+trading+emini
- ***The Economist (February 10, 2018) "In the Know: The Well Connected Really do Fare Better—Even During A Financial Crisis"*** (This article based on two studies asserts that Insider Trading is rampant).

- [Andrew Aziz, How to Day Trade for a Living](#)

Lloyd R Free

The author received a PhD from the University of Kansas and taught at the University of Michigan. He has published numerous articles on 18th-century French licentious literature and books including: *Virtue, Happiness and Duclos' "Histoire de Madame de Luz"* and *Laclos: Critical Approaches to "Les Liaisons Dangereuses", Confessions of a Day Trader*. He is currently working on a new novel celebrating the beatnik jazz and poetry scene in San Francisco and Paris, circa 1960.

Website: http://www.lloydfreeauthor.com/

Express Yourself

Your opinion matters. If you found this lexicon helpful, please write a brief review and post it to Amazon.com or Goodreads.com. I thank you in advance and appreciate you taking the time to rate this primer. If you found the idea of day trading interesting or if you are a day trader or investor, then perhaps you should visit the Amazon page for Confessions of a Day Trader and consider purchasing the book. It is available in both paperback and digital versions. I always appreciate your feedback.